Ll

Lunch

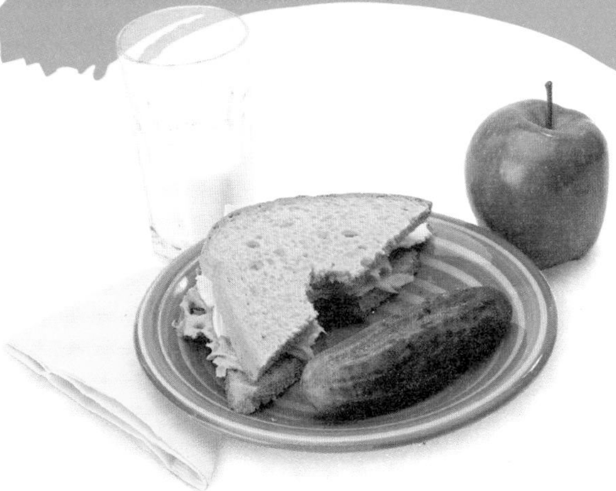

Written by Leslie Ellen

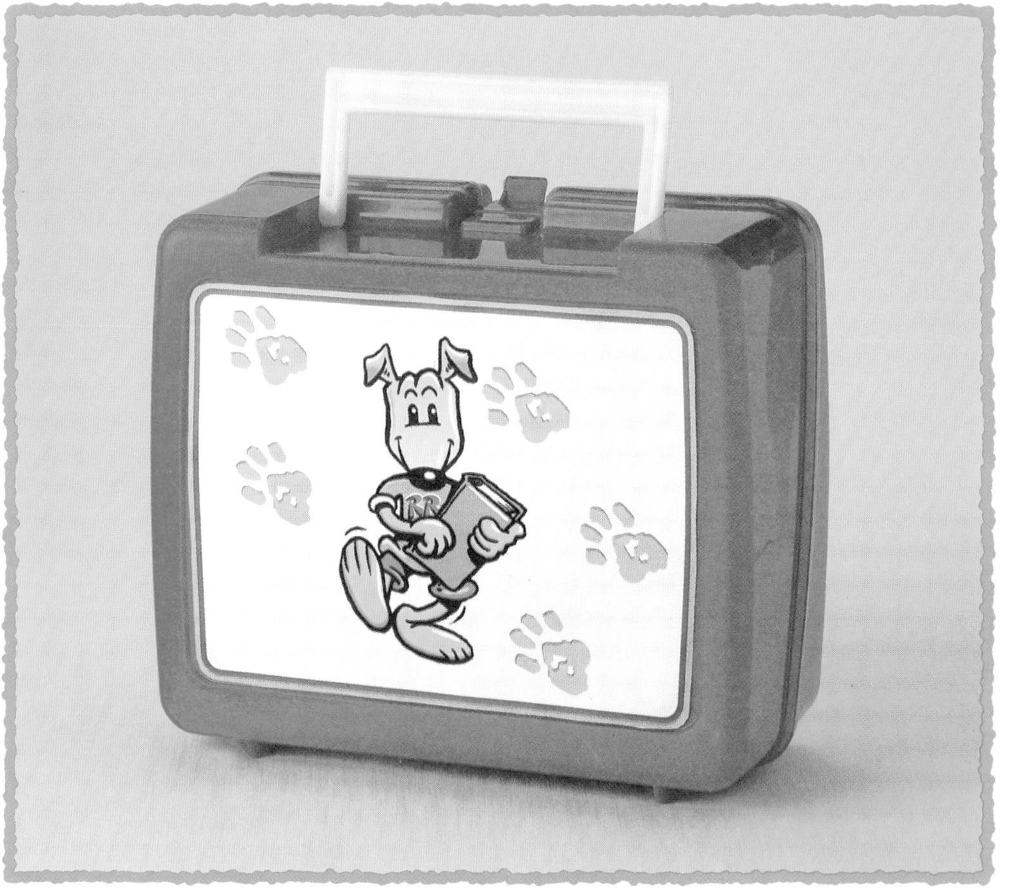

lunch box

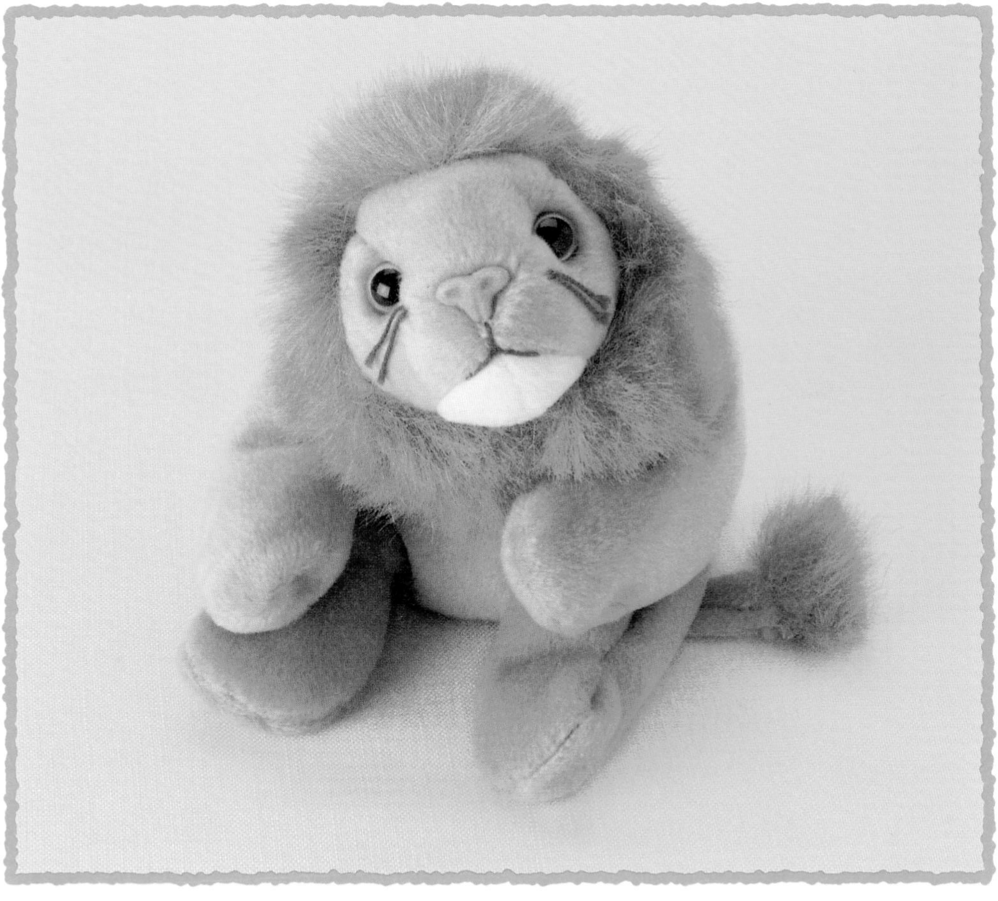

lion

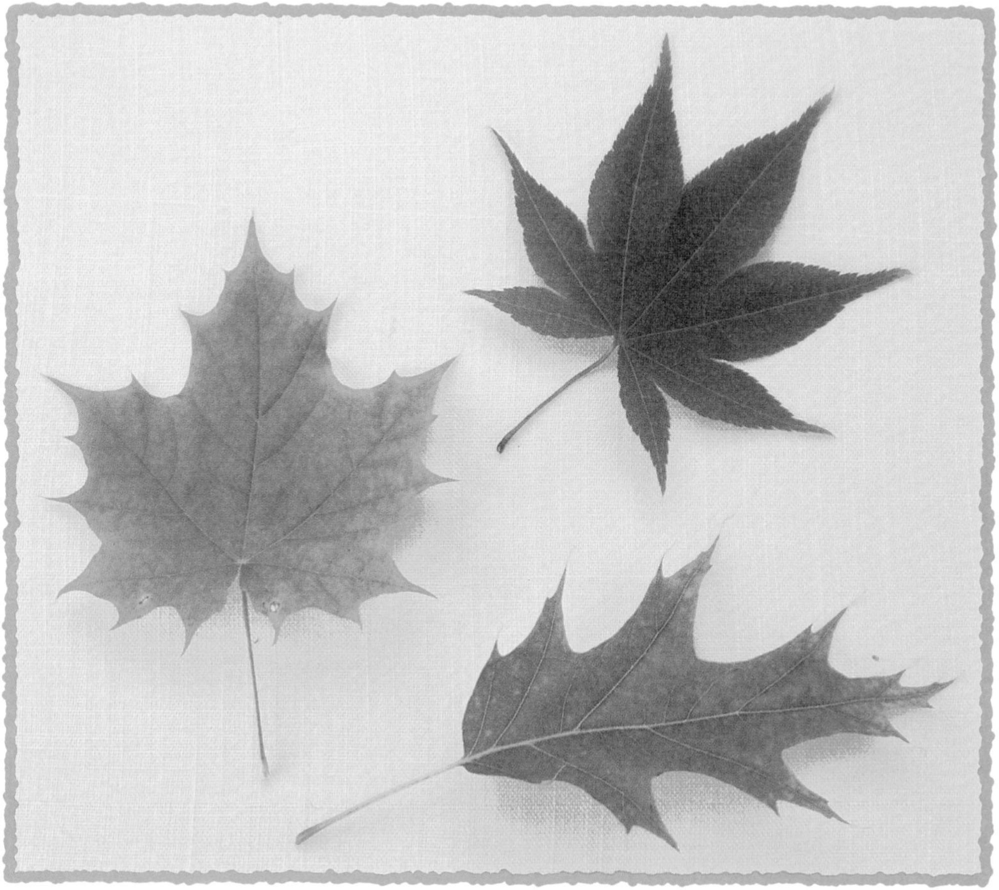

leaves

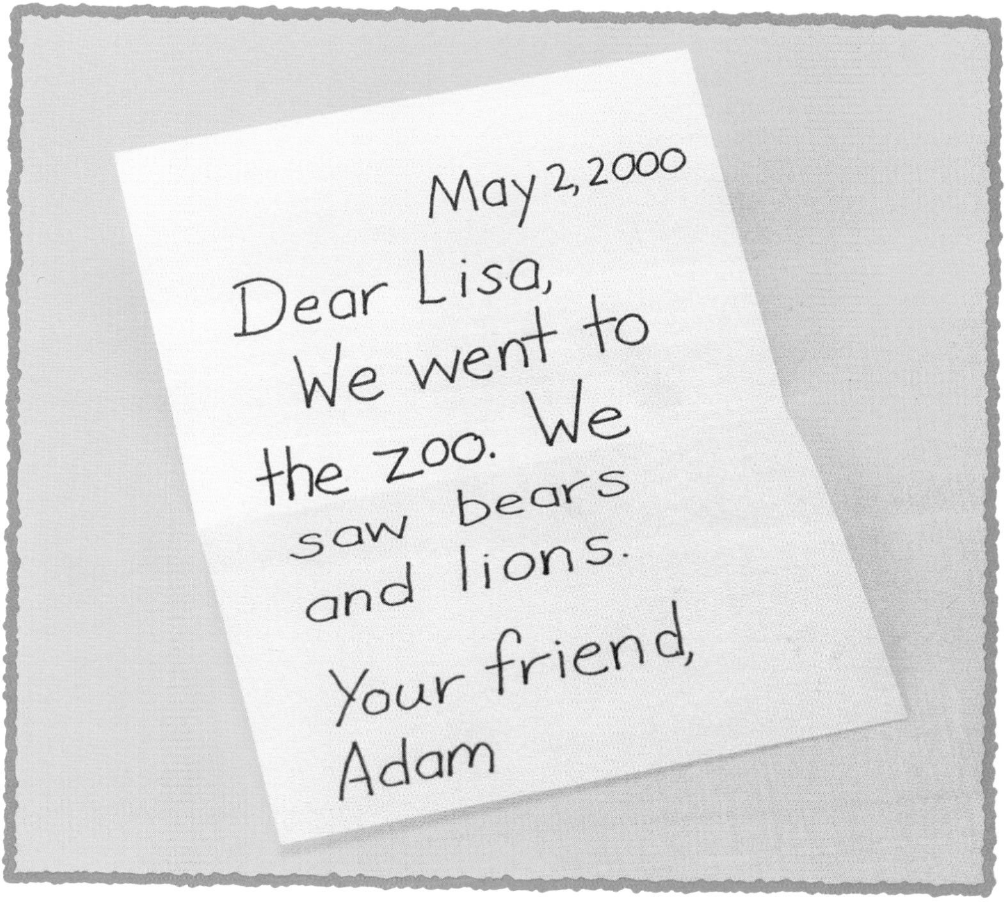
May 2, 2000
Dear Lisa,
We went to
the zoo. We
saw bears
and lions.
Your friend,
Adam

letter

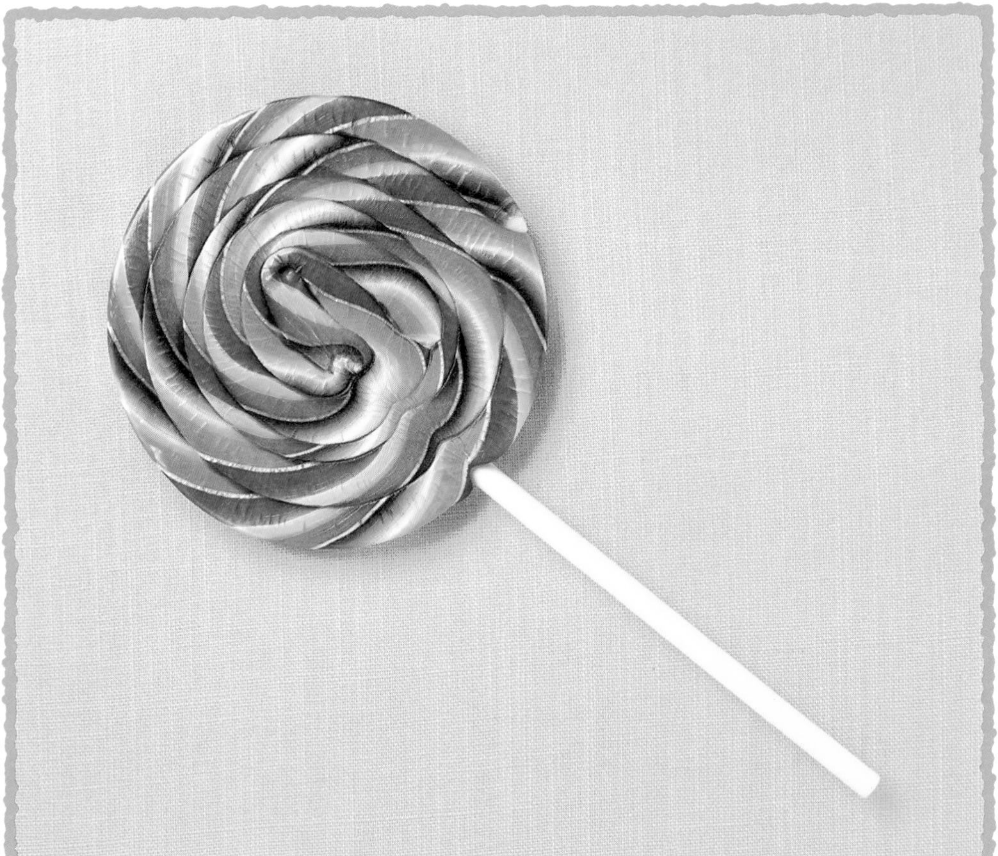

lollipop

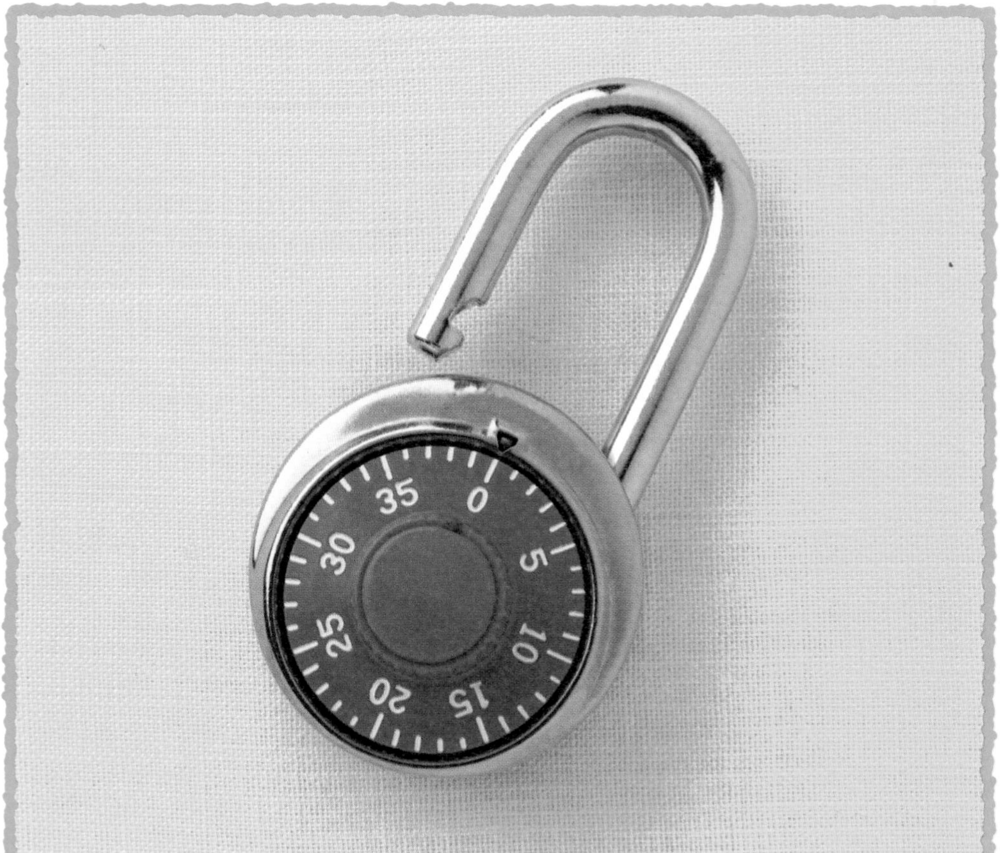

lock

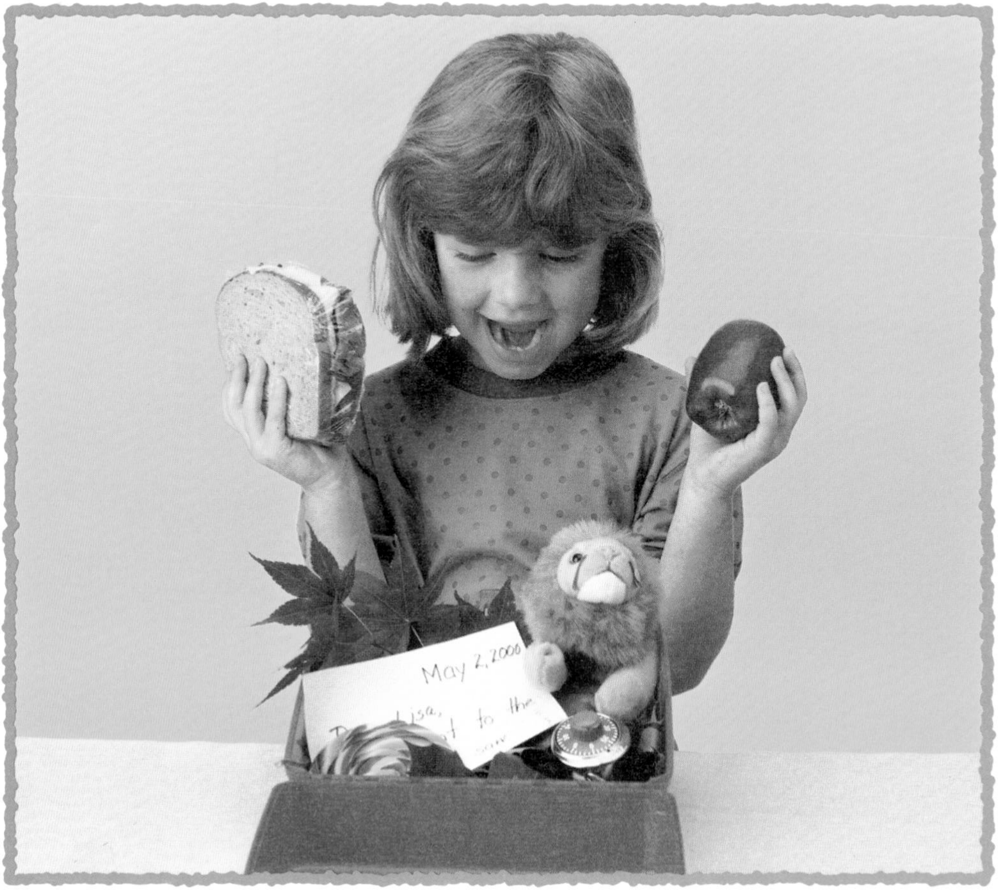

Lunch?